Essie

Essie

The True Story of A Teenage Fighter
In The Bielski Partisans

Essie Shor and Andrea Zakin

MINDFULNESS PUBLISHING
www.essieshor.com

Cover Design by: Accurance Inc.
Interior Design by: MyLinda Butterworth of Day to Day Enterprises

ISBN-13:   978-0-9821844-5-5 Clothbound
ISBN-13   978-0-9821844-4-8 Trade Paper

Printed in the United States of America
10 9 8 7 6 5 4 3 2 1

Publisher's Cataloging-in-Publication data

Shor, Essie.
    Essie : the true story of a teenage fighter in the Bielski partisans / Essie
Shor and Andrea Zakin.
    p. cm.
    ISBN 978-0-9821844-5-5
1. Shor, Essie. 2. Holocaust survivors --Biography. 3. Jews--Persecutions--
Belarus. 4. Holocaust, Jewish (1939-1945)--Belarus--Personal narratives.
5. World War, 1939-1945 --Jewish resistance --Belarus. 6. World War,
1939-1945 --Jews --Rescue --Belarus. 7. World War, 1939-1945 --Jewish
resistance --Biography. I. Zakin, Andrea. II. Title.

DS134.72.B79 .S56 2009
940.53/18092--dc22   2008942180

Mindfulness Publishing
PO Box 353
Bryn Mawr, PA 19010

610-955-2468
www.essieshor.com

11 09

*In Memory of my daughter Celia,
and my husband Jerry,
and all of those who lost their lives
in the Holocaust.*

About the Authors

Essie Shor

After a year enslaved in the ghetto of her home town of Novogrudek, where most of her family was killed by the Nazis, teenage Essie Shor daringly escaped. She spent the next two years in the forest encampment led by her cousins, the Bielski Brothers, and became a partisan, a guerrilla fighter attacking the Nazi war  machine. Following the war, she married Jerry Shor after a one-month courtship, and moved with her husband and two-year-old daughter to New York, where she had a second daughter. Essie worked for a major book manufacturer, and eventually became a public school teacher, retiring at age 80. She lives in New York.

Andrea Zakin

 A professor at Lehman College, taught an early childhood education class that Essie attended at Lehman College in the Bronx. This book came out of an art project Essie did for Andrea's class, representing her life in the forest bunker. Andrea suggested that Essie write this story for young adult readers because it would represent a unique perspective on this aspect of the war from an adolescent's point of view. And so began the collaboration—at first between teacher and student, and then between co-authors and friends. Andrea is also a widely known painter, who uses her art to comment on political and social issues. She lives with her husband and teenage daughter in New York.

Acknowledgments

$\mathcal{I}$ would like to express my gratitude to the following people:

Essie

The Bielski family for their love and support throughout the writing of this book. Mickey Bielski for always patiently listening to my story and being there for me. His brother Robert Bielski for understanding me and helping me to get "out of my own way." Ed Zwick and Paramount Vantage for bringing Nechama Tec's book, "Defiance," to life in an extraordinary movie, also called "Defiance"—and honoring me along the way. Peter Duffy, author of a great book, "The Bielski Brothers," for his insight, encouragement, and gentle manner. Chris Bielski for her kindness and for graciously sending me a copy of *Escaping Into the Night*.

D. Dina Friedman, whose novel *Escaping Into the Night* made it clear that there is still interest in this hidden story of the Holocaust, and who connected us with her husband, book shepherd and marketing consultant Shel Horowitz of FrugalMarketing.com. Shel steered us through the complicated process of making a book and cleared the way to approach several important connections. Sarah Doyle's editing smoothed out the rough edges and made the story come alive. MyLinda Butterworth of Day to Day Enterprises surpassed our wildest dreams with her beautiful interior design, and the stunning cover was created by Accurance.

Ruth Bielski's son, Brendon Rennert who took an interest in seeing that the photos in this book would be part of the Florida Holocaust Museum Exhibit. Erin Blankenship, curator of the museum, and the Bielski family for giving me permission to reprint these pictures. Lola Kline for dictating her amazing childhood story that is now part of my book. Barbara Lipensky for getting so much of the work ready for publication by sitting with me and my computer for weeks.

In writing this book, I have consulted with many who gave such good advice and support, Ron Schonfeld, Dr. Ken Harris, and of course my bright and talented grandchildren, Chad, Alix and Carly. Dr Oz, cardiothoracic surgeon, who advised me to have my open heart surgery last year and after I told him I was a partisan and a survivor said " You were a partisan, then you're going to survive and tell your story".

A huge thank you to my co-author Andrea Zakin, who believed so strongly in my story that she made it real. She has been amazingly supportive through the many years that we have been working together.

My daughter, Lora Shor, whose constant prodding and encouragement brought my story to life. She coordinated the work of everyone involved in this project, listened to me endlessly, and actually created a publishing company to bring my words to print. Without her love, time and energy, this book would not have been possible.

Andrea

I wish to thank my husband, Taka, and my daughter, Kimi, as well as my readers and friends, Abigail McNamee, Laurie and Art Sherman, and Diane Lorber (and her class) for their feedback and support. I especially wish to extend my thanks to Essie, whom I met serendipitously so long ago, and who never gives up no matter what. I have learned so much from working on this project together. I also wish to thank Essie's daughter, Lora, for helping to bring this project to fruition.

ONE

The Nazis Arrive

When I was sixteen years old, my happy childhood years suddenly disappeared as if they'd been a dream from another life. The Germans had invaded Poland, the country had been split in two, and the war came to my town. I was forced to grow up very quickly.

My small city of Novogrudek was in what is now northeast Belarus, but when I lived there, it was still a part of Poland. Even in the 1930s, when my present home of New York City had skyscrapers and modern industry, historic Novogrudek still had horses pulling buggies along cobblestone streets and a maze of small wooden houses interconnected by courtyards.

The town had many old, imposing buildings, including ancient churches and synagogues. The venerable old synagogue my family and neighbors attended was the center of our lives, an elegant yet monumental stone structure with a soaring vaulted ceiling that I regarded with awe from the women's balcony during Saturday services.

We heard about the war over the radio in the summer of 1939. We learned that the German armies were fighting a war against many countries, and spreading into Poland that September.

When the Germans invaded in 1939, they and the Russians split the country between them at first. Germany took the west and the Russians took the east, where Novogrudek lay. Later, the Germans would break their treaty with Russia and invade our part of Poland, too.

We were even a little relieved to be taken over by the Russians in the partition, since the Nazis believed only in the superiority of their own race and creed. They wanted everyone to look the same: fair coloring, preferably blond hair and blue eyes. Anyone who was not like this particular kind of German was considered different, and to be different was to be despised as inferior.

Jews and other groups were different, and hated. My family was Jewish. I was Jewish. So why were the Nazis fighting me—I was barely more than a child? They wanted to dominate Poland and control Polish land, even if it meant killing people, especially Jews, but we only understood this part later. At the time, all we knew was that we were in danger. Many Christians lived in Novogrudek, and still do. Many Jews used to live in Novogrudek, but few do now.

My family lived with our neighbors in a small Jewish community where everyone was poor, so nobody thought much about it. We didn't have bathrooms or indoor plumbing, but used outhouses. Children washed the dishes in water that we lugged in from the pump outside and heated over a wood-fired oven. The wood came from nearby villagers, who hauled it by horse and wagon to sell to the people in town.

Our family got along well together. We had the usual squabbles but also much laughter and talk at the dinner table. I always thought my parents made a good team. Even during the terrible times that came, I felt protected by them. My mother helped my father, a bookbinder, by gathering books from offices, libraries, students, even the private homes of wealthy people, and my father would repair or replace their bindings at his worktable in a corner of the dining room.

My youngest sister, Mariashke, was a fair-haired, well-behaved child who enjoyed playing quietly with her dolls. Rivale, the blond and rosy-cheeked middle sister, was more outgoing, always singing and playing with the other neighborhood children. The younger brother, whom we called Archik, the nickname for Aron, was already studious at age 14. After his bar mitzvah at the traditional age of 13, he became religious and kept more and more to himself. I came next, age 15, with hazel eyes and blond hair. The oldest was Israel, who was 18. He had grown tired of book learning and instead pursued a trade repairing sewing machines, typewriters, and bicycles. Israel and I often argued with each other, perhaps because we were most alike.

I miss them all to this day.

Every night, families like ours gathered around their radios to listen. Every day, people gathered in small groups to try to make sense of what they had heard the night before. It was all that people talked about. It was all that we thought about. Over the months that followed, we heard rumors that several small neighboring towns had been bombed and occupied by the German army. Some Jews from these towns managed to escape to Novogrudek seeking safety, but the bombing came to us as well.

Late one afternoon in July 1941, we heard the sound of bombs that could only be coming from somewhere in our own town. Neighbors up and down the street ran out of their houses crying, "War! The war has come to us!" We were home that day. My father, as usual, was at his table in the corner peeling the cover off an old book to prepare it for a new binding.

My mother reacted first. Thinking fast, she shouted, "Take all the valuables and throw them in the *sklep!*" She meant the underground cooler, also called a *pivsnica*, that served as a refrigerator in the basement of our old-fashioned house. My brothers, sisters, and I ran around the house grabbing pots, pans, candlesticks, and even a live, flapping fish, and quickly threw them all into the sklep. We then fled to the orchard of Christian neighbors who lived on the next street, hoping it would be safer there.

When the bombing stopped, it was eerily silent. We were grateful that our house had not been hit, but we were still frightened while we waited to see what would happen next.

 TWO

Hanukah as Refugees

We did not have to wait long to hear that the Nazis had ordered Jews—not Christians—to bring everything of value that they owned to the town square. We saw their sign warning that Jews in other towns had been killed when they did not hand over enough or if they tried to keep anything back, so we gave everything we had. Although poor, most of us had a few treasured items that had been passed down from generation to generation.

My parents regretfully parted with silverware, vases, candlesticks, the silver goblet used ritually at the Passover Seder, their gold wedding rings, everything. So did all the other Jews in town. This is how we lost, within a matter of days, pieces of family history that held the memory of who we once were.

Our lives completely changed. At first, we were in a state of shock, but gradually, we got used to it. We no longer went to school, carrying satchels of books and lunches wrapped in stiff paper, our brown, hard-heeled shoes echoing down the cobblestone streets; Jewish children were not allowed to go to school. We no longer ran shrieking gleefully in a game of tag through the tangle of courtyards that connected our homes, nor played hopscotch with bits of broken glass salvaged from broken crockery; Jewish children spent their time trying to survive.

We learned to live from day to day. Food was hard to come by. My family used whatever money we had to buy food from nearby farmers, but other families had to trade blankets and clothes in order to eat. We children went scouting for wood so we could cook and keep warm by the stove. Some neighbors were helpful. Later, they would not be.

My parents thought that we had a better chance to survive outside the center of town, so we borrowed a horse and wagon and rode out to my Uncle Yoshke's on the outskirts of Novogrudek—a large, airy, comfortable home with trees, flowers, and vegetables in a surrounding garden. Once we got there, though, my mother and father decided to move farther still, so my uncle and aunt, my aunt's mother, and my two young cousins piled into our wagon and we drove out to the Bielski homestead, another aunt and uncle's house deep in the countryside. The Bielskis had eleven children— nine boys and two girls—yet they did not hesitate to invite us to stay. We had to sleep in the barn with some of the Bielski children, but we didn't mind because the straw kept us warm and it was comforting to be together.

As we prepared for bed that night, we were startled to hear my Aunt Bielke speak sharply to her three eldest sons. "Tuvia, Asael, and Zus," she said. "You cannot sleep. You must stand guard with your scythes."

The young men looked perplexed. "Why?" they asked. "Aren't we safe enough? We are fifteen miles from town. Surely no one will bother us here." Aunt Bielke gave no explanation, but firmly told them to maintain their positions, and they of course obeyed. Now I realize that she alone recognized the seriousness of our situation.

The next day, we left the Bielskis and returned home to collect some of our belongings. To our great shock, when we came upon our street we saw that the entire neighborhood had been completely destroyed. We searched through the wreckage that had once been our home and with a desperate sort of triumph retrieved our pots, pans, and, strangely, the fish, still alive in the sklep. Of course, we took the fish with us and ate it that night at my Uncle Yoshke's house. Our home and most of our belongings gone, we lived with Uncle Yoshke's family for the next six months.

The day after finding our fish in the sklep, I was passing through the marketplace on an errand for my mother when I noticed people from prominent Jewish families, teachers from the Jewish schools, and other professionals standing uncertainly together. On the way home, I looked for them again, thinking to greet my teachers with a curtsy, as we did as a sign of respect when we met them outside of school.

Instead, I found them all lying dead on the ground. I could not believe my eyes. Terror-stricken, I ran all the way home to Uncle Yoshke's, sobbing. My mother took me into her arms and held me, but said nothing. What could she say? I understood later that the Nazis made it their business to kill Jewish intellectuals first, knowing that educated people who think for themselves are more difficult to control.

Even living at Uncle Yoshke's house, surrounded by family, our fear deepened. In this frantic, frightening time, the beginning of a world war unprecedented in history, we had to believe that Jews had a chance of surviving if we did not anger the Nazis. We tried not to give them a reason to notice us. We tried to comply with their commands. We did not conceive that a nation would systematically kill us for no apparent reason. We had no idea that they meant to kill us, no matter what we did or did not do.

December came, bringing Hanukah, the remembrance of the ancient victory of a small band of Jews who fought the pagans to regain their beloved Jerusalem. It is called the Festival of Miracles and Lights because the Maccabees' Temple lights burned for eight days, although there was only enough oil to burn for one day.

We lit Hanukah candles Uncle Yoshke had saved from the time he owned a small grocery store. Watching Uncle Yoshke, I thought about how, before the war, on each of the eight nights of Hanukah, my family had gazed, rapt, as my father lit another candle and gently placed it in one of the eight holders in our old brass menorah (Jewish candelabra), which was then proudly displayed in the entryway window. It was a magical experience to walk down our street at night and view the candles flickering in every Jewish home. It made me feel special to be part of this community, a community of candles and light.

This year at Uncle Yoshke's, we were able to eat *latkes*, potato pancakes that my mother fried in oil and sprinkled with sugar on top. I can still taste my mother's latkes, they were that delicious! This year, we had no dreidel to play with, no Hanukah gelt (little coins wrapped in cloth), so family spirit had to compensate for the loss of the usual holiday festivities. I have a poignant memory of my young cousins dancing with my six-year-old sister Mariashke while we sang traditional Hanukah songs.

The handsome and charismatic Tuvia Bielski, far right, late 1930's. The two uniformed men are Polish Policeman. *Photo courtesy of Mickey Bielski*

Essie in Novogrudek. *Photo courtesy of the Shor family.*

THREE

Surviving the Massacre

A few days later, I was on my way home when I saw posters announcing that Jews were not to leave town and were supposed to remain at home at all times until further notice. I hurried home to tell my mother and my brother Israel, who had also just arrived back home from work.

Ever the bold thinker, Israel was decisive. "As soon as Aron and Father are home, we've got to go to the Bielskis," he said. "We can't let them trap us in our own homes!" We had heard that our Bielski cousins and a few other Jews had escaped to the forest and were living there.

As it turned out, Aron and Israel left without us that day, my mother promising we would follow shortly, as soon as Father got back. It was winter, and she wanted to prepare at least a little. We kissed them goodbye and wished them luck. However, by the time my father came home and we left our house, the town was surrounded by police and we had to go back. I anxiously hoped that my brothers had been fast enough to get past the police blockade.

Soon, all the Novogrudek Jews were again called to the town courthouse, where we had given over our most valued belongings a few months before. Formerly, we had regarded the grand brick and stone structure with pride, but now we didn't know what to think, except to be afraid. Wanting to feel prepared, yet not knowing what we were preparing for, we wore as many clothes as we could, one piece on top of the other.

As my family walked together toward the courthouse, we saw other Jewish families proceeding to the same destination. There was a hush in the air. Everyone was scared. Everyone was thinking their own thoughts, afraid to say them aloud. What had happened to neighbors who were missing but never mentioned? Had they really been killed, as we had heard? I couldn't avoid thinking of my brothers and wished fervently that they had reached our Bielski cousins in the woods.

When we arrived at the courthouse, we were stunned by what we saw. Some people were weeping, while others sat absolutely still, staring straight ahead. Children were crying from hunger. My family stood awkwardly together, uncertain what to do, until we found an open space on the floor and squeezed into it. Several people noticed a chimney in the room and made a fire. My mother cooked oatmeal cereal that we shared with other children. It was winter and very cold, but because so many people were packed in together and everyone was wearing so many clothes, we were able to keep warm. The children slept that night while the weary but sleepless grownups watched, wondered, and waited.

The Nazis came in the morning. They wore high shiny boots and wide leather belts with huge buckles on which was written, "Gott mit uns" (God is with us). They never looked at us and never smiled.

Families with young children, like ours, were sent out to the courtyard. My father and I were standing in the courtyard behind my mother and sisters when a Nazi guard killed a young girl and lifted her lifeless body into an army vehicle. My throat closed up and my knees began to shake violently. I whispered to my mother, "Let's move to the back of the crowd. I want to live a little longer." My sister Rivale, then ten years old, must have seen the same thing, because she pleaded, "Will they really kill us?"

There was no time to answer her. A high-ranking Nazi officer suddenly marched in. I recognized him, because my father used to bind books for him. Without thinking, I ran up and grabbed onto his sturdy belt buckle, pleading, "My father is the only bookbinder in town. You will need him!"

The officer didn't even look at me. "*Ja,*" he said, "*wir brauchen ihn*" ("We will need him"). He yelled to my father, "Bookbinder, come here!" My father ran out from the crowd to join me. I distinctly remember people begging us, "Tell them I'm your mother, your sister, your grandfather ..."

Another Nazi officer commanded a young German soldier to push my father and me back into the courthouse. On an impulse, I quickly turned around to the soldier and, standing on tiptoe, planted a kiss on his ruddy cheek. I hoped it would persuade him to include the rest of my family, waiting vulnerable and frightened outside in the courtyard.

This small act, born of frantic desperation and childish hope, enraged another soldier standing nearby, who charged my father and smashed him in the head with his gun, screaming *"Rassenschade!"* ("Racial sin," the supposed crime of contact with Jews). To the gendarme I had just kissed, now stiff with terror, he threatened, "You will be killed like a Jew!" The young soldier remained frozen, poisoned by the kiss of an outcast, a young Jewish girl.

Somewhere in this chaos, I remember my Uncle Yoshke's mother-in-law crying out to the German soldiers, "These are *meine Kinder*, they should come with me!" *Meine Kinder*, my children: she had used the German words in the hope of reaching his heart, but the surly gendarme was indifferent and only grunted in response, *"Gehen sie nach draussen wit ihren kindern"* ("So, go outside with your children."). Thus, my Uncle Yoshke joined his wife, children, and mother-in-law in the courtyard instead of coming with my father and me.

My father and I were roughly steered inside the building and down steep stairs to a damp, foul-smelling basement. Figures with faces difficult to decipher in the dark backed away from us in horror; they must have seen the blood streaming down my father's face. Isolated and in shock, my father and I stared hollowly at the surrounding group.

Only then, in a surge of anguish and despair, did I comprehend what had just happened. In the scenario played out in the courtyard, my father and I had been spared, and my mother and sisters had been lost and would die. I was overwhelmed by violently opposing feelings: relief because my father and I were alive and searing grief because my mother and sisters were certainly gone, and Uncle Yoshke and his family, too. Perhaps they were already dead.

I thought of little Mariashke's dolls and Rivale's lovely voice, of my mother's beautiful chestnut hair pulled into a bun at the back of her head. I suffer this guilt even now, the survivor's unbearable burden carried along with the selfish but deeply human feeling of gratitude that comes from being spared.

Later, I learned that the Nazis killed 4,000 people along with my family that day. My father and I were the only ones who survived this massacre outside the courthouse. We joined the rest of the about 700 Jews who were already in the courthouse, chosen to live by the Nazis before the outdoor massacre began.

Essie *Photo courtesy of the Shor family.*

FOUR

The Ghetto

*M*y father and I, along with the others in the courthouse, were herded into open army trucks and driven outside of town to the ghetto. We were instructed that this was the only place where we would be allowed to live, in old, one-story wooden houses sectioned off from the rest of the town by a high barbed wire fence capped with spikes. There was only one gate, guarded day and night by police. Seeing this prison, I was numb with fear as the truck rumbled through the heavily guarded gate. I felt my life was over, yet I was almost beyond caring. This would be my home for the next year.

The German soldiers roughly prodded us with their guns into the houses, counting heads like cattle, a certain number allotted to each. Each house consisted of four sizable rooms that were forced to hold ten people each, so forty to a house. Fortunately, my Uncle Shmuel, Aunt Elke, their sons Eshae and Reuben, and their daughter Miriam were steered in with us, so we were together. My Uncle Shmuel

Oppenheim was a machinist, probably spared because the Nazis considered his work useful to them. Others in our house included several acquaintances from my hometown, plus a few strangers who mostly kept to themselves at first. We looked around us. Everything looked foreign, as if we were in a strange country or even another world. It was unreal.

For a long time, I felt disconnected to life. The houses were old and dreary, with sooty, peeling wallpaper of brown, gray, and beige. The winter air was freezing cold, particularly in the mornings. Ghetto life became our new reality. It had its own rhythms, rules, and unspoken but well-understood patterns of behavior. We learned to wait our turn for everything from cooking and washing to fetching water from the pump to visiting the outhouse. I washed myself scooping water from a bowl and learned how to clean clothes without a washboard, scrubbing my hands raw. We washed our clothes on Sundays and dried them on a string stretched over our beds.

My father and I were lucky to have our own single beds attached to the wall, my father taking the top bunk. The others slept one next to the other on adjoining bunks, so everyone woke up when one person turned over.

Each house had a kitchen containing an old cement wood-burning stove and a huge brick oven for baking. I recall how just a glimpse of the coals glowing in an opened stove door made me feel warmer.

Families cooked for themselves. My battered pot of potato and barley soup was often pushed to the back burner where it was hard to get at, but I was thankful to have my potatoes and barley when I remembered the meager ration of bread and watery soup that the Germans provided in the communal kitchen. Jews who had nothing to barter had to settle for the slim pickings there, but my father and I usually managed to eat our own food in our house. We had a few things to barter, starting with the old clothes that we had worn in so many layers on that terrible day when we'd left for the courthouse.

Barter took the place of money in the ghetto and sometimes made the difference between life and death. It brought the food needed for survival, but it was illegal and therefore dangerous. An old shirt for a few onions: our exchanges revealed that Jews needed food while the town dwellers needed clothing.

Someone with something to barter would walk close to the fence that separated the ghetto from the outside world and peek through the wooden slats. If someone was on the other side—a mother, even a child, furtively glancing around to make sure that nobody was coming—a few muffled whispers made the terms of trade and the deed was done as quickly as possible. Anything large that had to be thrown over the fence compounded the danger. Large or small, speed was crucial, because anyone caught bartering faced serious trouble, even death.

Although I often had to barter, I preferred my father to do it. He was faster than I and commanded more respect. I was usually so scared that it was hard to think straight, and I sometimes settled for less food than I should have at a time when every bite mattered. In our house, we eyed each other's food with longing, but of course, we would not steal. It was a temptation new to me, but this was a life-and-death existence and our hunger was very real.

Stealing food was strictly forbidden by the *Judenrat*, the Jewish leadership council of the ghetto. Its members were educated professionals or elders on whom we relied for wisdom and justice. They made laws for ghetto dwellers and judged who was right or wrong when problems arose. Responsible for the smooth functioning of the ghetto, their reward was having better jobs and their own building to live in.

However, the Nazis gave orders directly to the Judenrat, so that the council was sometimes forced to decide who would live and who would die to fill a Nazi quota. Judenrat members were also the direct targets of Nazi wrath and blame, held accountable when there were problems. At times, they paid with their lives. Even friends and associates might be taken with them, so knowing someone in the Judenrat could help you, but it could also get you killed.

With so many people living in one room, I was never alone. We all had to try to get along with each other and live without privacy. Before the war, I could sit by myself dreaming private dreams, but now it was better not to think too much, if I could help it.

My father and I grieved for my mother, sisters, and brothers in our different ways. My father tried to hide his grief, but he had aged far beyond his forty years. Mine took a different physical form. Sometimes I was so sad that it caused a sharp, insistent pain in my chest. It hurt so much that my father took me to a doctor living in the ghetto, who examined me and reported that there was nothing the matter, except that I was suffering from grief.

In a strange way, the Nazi labor system came to my rescue, as I was soon put to work with a team of other girls to retrieve bricks from bombed-out buildings. It was strenuous work, but it kept me from thinking about my family. Slowly, I came back to life.

What helped most was prayer. The Germans strictly forbade us to have a synagogue, but each morning before we went to work, my father and I would say a few prayers, perched on the edge of our bunk beds. Saying our own prayers strengthened us.

I missed celebrating Hanukah and Passover, my two favorite holidays. When the Jewish holidays came around, we heard that small groups were gathering to celebrate, but we didn't join them because we were too busy trying to survive. Most of all, I missed celebrating with my family as we used to.

We always had to be vigilant. People left and did not reappear, but we kept our fears to ourselves. Rumors continually circulated: There would be a military "action" in two weeks … a week … soon. The main topic of conversation was trying to figure out the Nazi mentality and predict what they would do next. Of course, this was impossible, because no sane person could understand the way they thought.

All Jews, even children, had to wear the Star of David on our frayed woolen jackets. The star was yellow so it could easily be seen, so whenever we left the ghetto to work outside, everyone could immediately identify us as Jews.

It seemed as if new laws to limit our freedom were enacted every day, until there was no freedom left. Even thinking seemed forbidden.

I became too tired and numb to care, yet we all had to remain aware of each new rule so we would not make a fatal mistake. Each morning when my father trudged off to work, I wondered if I would see him again. I worried incessantly because I knew of men who left the ghetto for work in the morning and had not returned at night. My father worried about me, too. We all lived with constant fear while we occupied ourselves with the business of staying alive.

One day, we learned that Jews were not allowed to walk on the sidewalk outside of the ghetto. We were forced to pick our way among the horses and cattle on the cobblestone streets, as if we had become animals ourselves. Polish children who had once been my schoolmates passed us by as if we did not exist. I gazed at them with longing, wondering what it was like to walk blithely down the street without fear, as I had done once upon a time myself, in another existence long ago.

It hardly seemed possible that I had ever washed and ironed my white collared shirt each night to prepare for school the next day. I could hardly believe that I had sat at my desk in the classroom, wiping the excess ink from my pen before forming careful letters on the page in front of me, letters that had flowed into words and sentences and paragraphs that made perfect sense in a rational world.

All Jews who were not too old or too sick worked. We awoke early in the cold, dark morning and dressed quickly so as not to bother others still sleeping. Just after 6:00, a straggly line of shabbily dressed Jews could be seen treading silently down the main street of the ghetto, through the gate and into the hostile world outside. To pass through the gate, each worker had to be ready with work permit and printed place of employment, and the yellow Jewish star had to be visibly displayed on our jackets. Guards studiously checked each ghetto dweller in the morning and then again 12 hours later at night. Although all our work was exhausting, it was better to work because it occupied your mind. It might prolong your life, too, not only because it kept you from thinking too much, but because as long as you were useful to the Nazis, they would let you live.

Essie. *Photo courtesy of the Shor family.*

FIVE

Work

The few children who lived in the ghetto missed out on what it should mean to be young, that is, to play and have friends. I knew one girl named Henya, a pretty girl with dark curly hair, because she had lived three houses away from us in Novogrudek. It was a rare pleasure to talk with a girl my own age, and whenever we could, we reminisced about our old lives as if we were old people looking back on a distant childhood. Henya came from a wealthy, educated family. In fact, her father was a member of the Judenrat.

Through their contacts, I met the Foltanskis, a Polish couple who had applied to the Germans for household help. Henya and I were both selected to try out for the job, but I was chosen. Henya's father found her something else to do. Perhaps the Foltanskis saw in me a strong, willing worker. Jews from more privileged backgrounds often had a difficult time because they were not accustomed to hard work, but luckily, I was used to it.

I became part of that tired band of workers passing back and forth through the gate each day. This was my first job, and although Jews were not paid for their work, I did get to eat at the Foltanski's house, which was worth a lot. Mr. Foltanski was an engineer, tall, thin, distinguished-looking, with dark hair and a stern expression. He spoke with a low, firm voice.

When I first saw him, I thought, "Oh no, not another Nazi!" Nevertheless, he turned out to be a humane man. Because he built bridges for the Germans, he mingled with them and sometimes passed along valuable information about their intentions. Mr. Foltanski's advice helped keep me out of trouble. He once pointedly warned me not to become involved with the Judenrat because he heard that several members were to be killed.

Mrs. Foltanski was a capable and beautiful woman with blond wavy hair, a kind person who had compassion for this young Jewish girl. I always felt safe with her.

One morning, we went to market together. Searching for decent vegetables, I suddenly stopped and stared, for there before me was a young Polish man busily unloading some grain to be sold. I knew this man had to be from Rabniki because I recognized the jacket he was wearing: it was my brother's faded brown sheepskin jacket.

I had heard through the ghetto grapevine—we were not allowed newspapers or radios—that my brothers had never made it to the safety of the forest. They had decided to wait for us in the village of Rabniki and spent the night there in a Jewish home, arising very early the next morning to leave.

They were caught by a policeman; a German soldier then shot them and threw their bodies into a ditch. The man in the marketplace must have stolen the jacket from Israel before he was killed—or even peeled it from his body after he was dead. I could not stop myself.

Enraged, I strode over to him screaming, "You are wearing a Jewish coat! It's my brother's!" Startled and suddenly fearful, the man turned and ran. Breathing fast, shallow breaths, I returned to Mrs. Foltanski, who never said a word, and we walked on. She could have scolded me for bringing attention to us and putting us in danger, but her silence told me that she understood my feelings and sympathized. Not everyone was so lucky with their employer.

I was fortunate indeed to work for the Foltanskis. It was indoors where it was warm, and the food, although plain, was sufficient. It was a treat to eat bread, a piece of farmer's cheese, and milk. The job was demanding. I was responsible for all the heavy housework, scrubbing floors, clothes, and bed sheets and washing the dishes. Although the Foltanskis were kind to me, I had to do the job just right. One day when I had been too busy to wash the kitchen floor, Mr. Foltanski angrily said, "Please see that this never happens again!"

On my return from work each day, I would sink down on my plank bed and try to gather the energy to make dinner. I wanted to have food ready for my father when he came home because I could see that he was much more exhausted than I was. During the day, while he ate his meager ration of food, I was eating my midday meal at the Foltanskis, much more plentiful than anything the Germans ever provided. Each time, I felt guilty because my father could not eat the same food as I, and I was not allowed to bring any home.

One day, I was surprised by my father's arrival at the Foltanskis. When Mrs. Foltanski told me that he was waiting for me in the next room, I had a feeling of foreboding. My heart pounding, I wondered what had happened. Why was he there? When I entered the room and my father saw the expression on my face, he became worried, and the same concern appeared on his face. "My Esia", he cried, "What's wrong?"

It turned out that there was nothing wrong, after all. It was simply that he had been working nearby and decided to pay a visit. It could have been like old times, a father spending time with his daughter, if not for the expressions on our faces that revealed the pervasive fear we carried, always waiting to surface. Still, it was a momentous occasion, for at Mrs. Foltanski's invitation, I was finally able to share my food with my father.

Unfortunately, after only a few months, I lost my job with the Foltanskis because of a new regulation stipulating that Jews could work only for Germans. Perhaps the Nazis feared that people who were not German-born would not be loyal to the Nazi cause and might even be sympathetic to their Jewish workers. They were right, of course, for the Foltanskis did help me survive.

My next job was working in the *koszary* ("koshary"), the Polish word for the German army barracks, on the outskirts of town, where my father also worked, and a half-hour walk from the ghetto. Sometimes on my daily trudge to work, I would imagine that I was a bird that could sail over and away from the Germans to a peaceful, happy existence in a far-off land. At other times, I would catch glimpses of normal, everyday life and remember with pain what my own life had been.

Townspeople stared at us, sometimes with curiosity and embarrassment but more often with contempt. I averted my eyes and watched them on the sly, not wanting to draw attention to myself and risk punishment; for I feared I might be killed if I so much as looked at them the wrong way. Such things had happened.

However, when I arrived at the barracks for work, my miserable present would blot out any wistful dreams or memories of my ordinary, safe past life, and reality would set in. I was part of a team of girls who cleaned the enormous, rectangular wooden structures that comprised the barracks. It was extremely hard work that entailed carrying endless pails of water hanging from a pole that pressed down hard on my shoulders. As I scrubbed floors and tables, I paid close attention to the German soldiers' jokes and banter, hoping to catch some news, but I never managed to hear any useful information.

Essie and Itka
photo courtesy of Essie Shor

SIX

Escape to the Forest!

T hough I no longer worked for the Foltanskis, they had kindly asked me to keep in touch, so I occasionally went to visit. However, one day, Mrs. Foltanski came to see me at the ghetto.

This was most unusual. Non-Jews never came because it was not safe. She was not allowed to come to our house, or even through the gate, so she asked a guard where I could be found. The guard must have been surprised at her boldness, but he told her to go along the fence to a certain point near where I lived and to ask someone there to go get me. We had to talk through the slats in the fence.

She anxiously whispered that she wished to help me. She had heard of a group of Russian fighters called partisans, people who banded together to fight. These particular partisans were prisoners of war who had escaped from the Nazis and now faced their former captors. Did I want to join them?

What should I do with this news? My father was with me, so I turned to him. "Will you go by yourself, a girl of sixteen?" he said. I could not think of leaving him and did not know how I would escape, so I thanked Mrs. Foltanski for her trouble but remained in the ghetto. Things were different now, though, because I knew a hope I had not known before.

I soon learned that there were not only Russian partisans, but Jewish ones, too. Russian partisans were mainly escaped prisoners of war, while Jewish partisans were civilians, some of whom had been trained in the Polish army in the days when Jews were accepted there.

When I discovered that there were Jewish partisans, I immediately wanted to join them. I knew that my Bielski cousins were hiding in the woods, but I did not know yet that they were the ones who had started the group of Jewish partisans.

It was dangerous to stay and dangerous to go. My brothers had died trying to leave and my mother and sisters had been slaughtered for staying behind. I did not know what to do. I kept wrestling with the decision, weighing the risk of leaving with the risk of staying in the ghetto.

One day when I was working in the army barracks, I learned that there was to be a German *actia*, or action. I knew what that meant: Jews would be rounded up at random, taken away, and killed. Badly frightened, I ran to the Foltanskis for help and entered their parlor with tears streaming down my face.

Mr. Foltanski said little, but led me to the little room that he used as his office, where a small handgun was always sitting on his desk. Without warning, he grabbed the gun and pointed it directly at my head, shouting, "I can kill you now! Who would stop me?" Shocked, I stopped crying. I knew he was not going to kill me; he wanted me to save myself. This was Mr. Foltanski's way of preventing me from returning to the ghetto. Perhaps he thought that if Mrs. Foltanski's approach had not worked, this would.

Mrs. Foltanski came with an armload of clothes to wear so I would not be recognized as a Jew. I removed my raggedy dress and my shapeless jacket bearing the Star of David and slipped on Mrs. Foltanski's clothes, a bright blouse and skirt with a blue blazer. When I was dressed, they looked at me, satisfied, and proclaimed, "With these clothes and your light hair, you don't look Jewish."

Many people, especially the Nazis, thought that all Jews looked the same. In this case, I was fortunate that I didn't fit the stereotype. With my light hair and the camouflage of the clothes, I had the confidence to leave their house, even knowing I would have to pass Nazi soldiers on the way. Mrs. Foltanski came with me part way, leading me to a nearby cornfield to hide until she could come to find me the following day. I realize now how brave she was to do this.

I remained in the field all night, hiding among the tall, ripe corn. It was the longest night of my life. I tried to calm myself by praying constantly so I would not be overwhelmed with despair. I hoped that God would hear and protect me. I repeated my prayer over and over all night long:

"Sh'ma Israel, Adonai Elohenu, Adonai echod." ("Hear, O Israel, the Lord is our God, The Lord is One.")

Towards morning, I fell asleep in the middle of the cornfield.

Around noon, I heard Mrs. Foltanski calling softly in Polish, "Esia, where are you?" I responded just as softly, "Here I am," and cautiously stood up so she could see me. Our eyes locked. She threw me a white cloth-covered package of food. Nothing more was said, but I knew that she was wishing me luck. She left as quickly as she had come and I never saw her again.

I was ravenous, so I immediately sat to wolf down the salami she had prepared. It was such a treat! I had not had food like this in a long time. I soon became unbearably thirsty, though, and realized that Mrs. Foltanski had forgotten to bring water. Afraid to leave the cover of the field, I waited until late afternoon. Then, summoning my courage, I headed for a nearby pump, murmuring, "Let them kill me, I have to drink some water!"

As I approached the road to reach the pump on the other side, I quickly glanced in both directions to check if the coast was clear and noticed an old house close by. Rather than cross the street and risk revealing myself, I made a quick decision to creep alongside the house to request a drink of water instead.

This turned out to be unfortunate. I knocked, and a stout, round-faced woman wearing a worn housedress and a scarf covering her blond hair opened the door and squinted at me. For a moment we both stood still and simply stared at each other. Her look quickly turned from surprise to suspicion. Instead of offering the customary metal cup of water, she turned around to reveal a few Polish policemen who just happened to be sitting in her kitchen behind her. What terrible luck. "Police," she cried out with self-righteous indignation, "A stranger is begging outside. She's wearing a blue coat. Get her!" I ripped off Mrs. Foltanski's blue blazer and took off as fast as I could.

I ran until I could run no further and threw myself into a ditch deep in a cornfield. I still felt parched for water, but I was more scared than thirsty. I heard gunshots and menacing Polish voices repeating, "Come out, come out, we'll find you anyway!" It was like some nightmarish game of hide-and-seek, only with death as the consequence. I lay in the cold dirt, holding my legs close to my body for warmth and trying to control the trembling. The voices finally went away. I was so frightened that I hid for two days, but finally, on the third day, I could last no longer. I needed to find someone who would help me.

Weak from exposure, hunger, and thirst, I stood up. To my amazement, there, just a few feet in front of me, although I had not heard her, was a sturdy young woman methodically cutting corn with a scythe. A second later, my amazement turned to astonishment when I recognized her as the kind teacher who had taught me how to knit and sew in third grade! I called out, "*Dzien dobry, Pani Fiedrowiczowa!*" ("Good morning, Mrs. Fiedrowiczowa!") She returned my greeting in surprise. How strange it must have been for her to see a young Jewish girl she knew from her class rising up from the corn!

Even before slaking my thirst, I wanted to know about the *actia*. "What happened to all the Jews in the ghetto?" I blurted out. She told me that some had survived and were still there. I felt a little relief and prayed that my father was among them. She scooped water from the pail at her feet and quickly offered the metal cup. It seemed like a gift from God! I drank deeply, unaware of anything other than the cold liquid streaming down my throat.

Saying she wished she could help me more, she then invited me to share her lunch. It must have been difficult for this teacher, who had so often assisted me in class, to be unable to aid me now, when my need was so desperate.

I told her that I wanted to contact my former next-door neighbor, whose son used to play with my brother Aron and so perhaps would be willing to help me. Mrs. Fiedrowichova agreed it was worth trying, but advised me to wait until evening. It was Sunday, she said, and without my yellow star, I looked like a Christian, but I was dirty, unlike Sunday churchgoers, and would attract attention.

I waited as long as I could. Late in the afternoon, when the light was dim, I stealthily arrived at my neighbor's house near my old home, where I had not been for such a long time. I knew her to be a welcoming person, but now even decent people were afraid to help Jews. Filthy with mud, I requested soap and water. She invited me in, but brought the soap and water to me at the door, mumbling with embarrassment, "Please leave as soon as possible." I could see that she, too, was petrified. She did not want to be caught helping a Jew, for punishment would be certain, and even death was a possibility.

As I was about to leave her house, two imposing Belarusian policemen strode in, dressed in military brown. I froze, terrified. More police! But happily, they were friends of my neighbor and I was reassured they would not harm me, so I relaxed. Then an idea came to me. Perhaps my luck had turned. Would they escort me back to the ghetto? Well, they agreed to do this, but only if I paid them 200 rubles! I promised that my father would pay; silently hoping he was still alive. When I arrived home with the two policemen, I was overjoyed to see that my father was indeed alive, and he was able to borrow the money to pay them. I was back with my father at last! I had been gone four days, but it felt like a much longer journey.

My time in the ghetto was coming to an end. I had never stopped thinking about the partisans, and it was clear that the time had come to join them.

To get to the partisans was not easy. They lived in the woods and sent trusted peasants called *legalschicks* to convince other Jews to join them in hiding. At first, they called only on young men who had served in the Polish army and knew how to fight, but they wanted to save as many Jews as possible, so later spread their net wider.

I again prevailed on my father to let me leave. This time, he agreed. The recent *actia* had been too terrifying, and now his friend Gutel Berkowski, a man who had been born in a nearby village, would be leading the way. Gutel was familiar with the area and would protect me, and my father knew that my Bielski cousins would accept me into the partisans. And like me, he understood, but didn't say, that I had a better chance of survival outside the ghetto than in it.

Thus it came about that one cold, snowy December night, four frightened, shivering Jews sneaked out of the ghetto through a hole cut in the fence: Gutel, two members of his family, and me. In the old snow, our footprints were indistinguishable from ones made earlier. My father refused to join us. He felt that he could not pay the high price of freedom at his age. He wanted the semblance of a home and a bed to sleep in, no matter how lacking in comfort. I didn't want to leave him, but the only path to freedom—maybe the only path to life itself—led away from the ghetto.

I was full of resolve and consumed with fear at the same time. Shaking but silent, the four of us cautiously left the ghetto, one after the other. We feared we would be caught and killed on the spot, but we were fortunate: no policemen found us and no one reported us. We walked fifteen long miles in the middle of the night along a narrow, winding country road partly hidden by trees, arriving hours later at an isolated house on the edge of the woods. A friend of the partisans named Koslewski was waiting for us, leaning casually against a tree. He led us single-file from the peasant's house into the forest. Branches slapped our faces and caught our clothes, but no one complained. In fact, no one uttered a word for hours, so engrossed were we in our escape. With every step, I began to feel free and hopeful in my heart.

At last, we walked into a clearing deep in the woods. As I peered into the dissolving morning mist, I discerned people sitting around an open fire shielded by the trees. They were singing hopeful songs of freedom in low voices. I glimpsed worn, heavy fabric slung over low-hanging branches to form primitive tents, reminding me of the joyful harvest holiday of Sukkoth. To this day, I can recall the sound of a murmuring brook mingling with the melody and harmonizing with their songs.

Asael Bielski
Photo courtesy of
The Bielski family

Tuvia Bielski
Photo courtesy of
The Bielski family

Zus Bielski
Photo courtesy of
The Bielski family.

SEVEN

The Bielski Partisan Encampment

hree blurry figures stepped forward out from the fog, and I recognized my cousins, Tuvia, Asael, and Zus! We hugged each other tightly. Wrapped in their broad arms, I felt safe for the first time in so long. Yet that night as I drifted off to sleep near the fire, its flames twisting in the strong winter wind, I wondered if my father, asleep indoors on his hard wooden bed, was safer than I, shivering in my bed of leaves in the forest.

The next morning when I awoke, stiff and cold, I counted two dozen people moving ghost-like in the early morning mist. I thought to myself, "Well, that makes a good sized family but a rather small army!" Nevertheless, that group of twenty-five was the kernel of the Bielski Partisan Brigade, which lived in the forest for three years and ultimately grew to over a thousand Jews! Now when I look back, I'm so proud that I was among the original members.

Seeing my cousins talking earnestly among themselves brought back memories of our weekly visits before the war. The Bielski family had owned an old, dilapidated mill on the edge of a lake surrounded by tall grasses and wildflowers, where villagers brought their grain to be ground into flour. Their rickety little wooden house had only a dirt floor, and there were so many children that several had to sleep in the barn, the same one where my family had slept the night that seemed so long ago now, when we fled the bombing of Novogrudek. I had always felt free at my Bielski relatives' home, warmly greeted by my aunt and uncle and their children.

Zus, the third brother, had often visited our house in Novogrudek. Several times a week, we would see him bicycling down the road toward us. As he neared our home, my mother would look up, nod, and add a few more potatoes to the pot.

I soon discovered that everybody respected the Bielskis. There were five of them in the partisans: The three oldest brothers were Tuvia, Asael, and Zus, and the youngest was Aron, age 12. Their sister Taiba and her husband were there, too.

The three oldest brothers in particular possessed a wide variety of skills learned from working alongside their parents. They knew how to repair houses and machinery, how to work with animals and grow food, and how to work together to get the job done. The Bielski brothers were all born leaders and had trained as soldiers in the Polish army. Anyone who met them respected them, and, when they had gotten to know them, trusted them.

Tuvia, the eldest, became our chief. He was a handsome man with dark curly hair and keen, thoughtful eyes. He stood tall and erect and was bold and courageous, yet capable of great kindness. His gentle ways and charismatic presence drew people to him. When Tuvia spoke, people listened, and when he gave a command, people obeyed. He had great foresight, inspiring our trust that he would keep us alive. To me, he had the noble bearing of a biblical hero.

Asael, the second oldest, was tall and strong, a fearless fighter who went on many dangerous missions. He was popular among the partisans because he listened carefully and helped people to solve their disagreements. He always acted like an older brother to me. That first winter, catching me shivering in a light coat, he removed his heavy woolen jacket and handed it to me saying, "Take it. Don't worry, I'll be fine." That jacket helped me survive outdoors that first long, cold, hard winter.

Carefree and easy-going as a youth, the third son, Zus, became a decisive partisan leader who commanded a unit of the bravest fighters, whose missions were to inflict damage on German army units and then quickly hide. Today we would call this kind of fighting guerilla warfare, but then people likened them to the Maccabees whom we celebrated at Hanukah. The Germans rarely caught Zus's men.

My cousin Taiba and her husband were distraught, for they had been forced to leave their 3-month-old baby, Lola, with Christian neighbors when the infant's crying had jeopardized everyone's safety in the woods. The child had been sick, too, and it was difficult to care for her in such wild and unstable circumstances.

They had arranged with a childless Catholic couple to leave their baby in the snow in an agreed-upon location, so the couple could pretend she had been abandoned and raise her as their own until the war was over. Lola was left with a note that said, "I am the daughter of a poor Christian and because of the war, my mother can no longer take care of me. To anyone who finds me, I beg you, please save me and bring me home with you and take care of me." Without the note, she surely would have been killed.

The couple reported to the police that they had found the baby and showed them the note. Unfortunately, neighbors also reported their suspicion that the child was a Jew. Baby Lola was examined and the Christian adoptive parents, the Kenceiziers, were interrogated twice more by the police, so they never felt secure that their secret was safe. When she was old enough to talk, they warned Lola to be careful of what she said around people outside the family, especially police and Germans—although they never told her that she was a Jew.

Like other children, Lola was repeatedly frightened by armed attacks and bombing raids. They often had to flee to the woods, where her adoptive parents would shelter her between them. Little Lola grew up in terror that she would be punished and killed by German soldiers and had nightmares of being trapped by them inside the grotesquely gaping hole in the ruins of the bombed-out family barn, which held a special horror for her..

Her Christian parents were kind and loving to her. Expecting that Lola's real parents would probably not survive the war, they'd had her baptized and raised her as a devout

Catholic. It was a terrible ache for Taiba and her husband to part from their child, but they saw no alternative.

For me, living with the partisans was the beginning of a new life. There was still hardship and fear, but also a kind of freedom, since there were no guards watching our every move. Living in the forest, we no longer felt like cattle, as we had in the ghetto.

However, we had to move constantly. There were German soldiers looking for us everywhere, and sometimes villagers living nearby would tell them where we were. Once, we had to leave in a hurry when the Nazis discovered the hoof prints of our cows in the snow. This was a different kind of fear. We went from being caged to being hunted.

At first we lived in the makeshift tents that I had spied the night I arrived. It was relentlessly cold! We slept close together for warmth and sometimes awoke to crackling clothes that had frozen on our bodies overnight. In the morning, we would make a fire to warm ourselves and to cook. Finding food was hard. We had no money, and it would have been hard to spend it even if we had had it. We never stayed in one place long enough to grow crops, and at this time of year the ground was frozen anyway.

We needed cows for meat and milk, so we had to take them from farmers and villagers who owned at least a few. At Tuvia's wise insistence, we never took everything, for the farmers also needed to survive. However, they did not give their animals to us willingly, of course. We had to resort to threats and lies. We proclaimed with bravado that we were members of a large army with plenty of ammunition who were capable of causing great destruction. We were hardly an army, only a motley group of undernourished, downtrodden souls, and only a few among us possessed military training or any knowledge of how to fight.

EIGHT

I Learn to Fight—and Non-Fighters Join the Partisans

*A*fter living in the forest for a month, I wrote my father a letter. It took a while to write and longer still to deliver. A few partisans secretly traveled to the ghetto to liberate Jews and maintain communication, so they occasionally carried letters back and forth between loved ones. I missed my father and worried constantly about him, wondering with dread when there would be another raid in the ghetto. I felt certain he would be safer with me in the partisan camp. I wrote the letter in such a direct way that my father could not ignore my message. I wrote:

Dear Father,

It is time for you to join me with the partisans here in the forest. Not only am I here, but your nephews and nieces as well. Tuvia is our leader, and Asael and Zus too. I know you will be safer with us. If you want to remain my father, you must come. If you do not come, then you can no longer be my father. I cannot sleep because I am so worried about you.

You are all I have left. Please come.
Your daughter, Essie.

Of course, he came!

On the day my father arrived, we stood talking in the peaceful quiet of the forest. Relief flooded over me, I was so happy we were together again, but this didn't last long. Suddenly, we heard several partisans yelling, "Run for your life, the Germans are coming!" and we had to make a mad dash for safety. As we ran, my father cried out, "Why did you bring me here, to die like a dog in a place where no one can bury me?"

I secretly reproached myself. "What have I done?" I thought. As it turned out, the alarm was an exercise in survival, a practice much like fire drills at school. The difference was that we were preparing for a *probna oblava*, a surprise attack by German Nazis who meant to kill us.

As time went by, even my father began to get used to the new life he had begun, and we had all had so many lives. Sometimes, we joined forces with a Russian partisan group, since we depended on the same resources for survival, the same food from the same farmers. This common problem sometimes created friction between the two groups. One time, a group of Russian partisans overcame 10 men from our *otriad* (unit of soldiers) and took away their rifles, saying that the Jewish partisans cared only about their own survival rather than about fighting the Germans.

Instead of either seeking revenge or remaining quiet, Tuvia brought members of our group to meet with the Russians.

"A bullet from a rifle in Jewish hands kills just the same as a rifle in Russian hands," he told them. The Russians respected him for this bold move and never again took away our rifles or bothered our partisans. When Tuvia told us about this encounter, we were filled with confidence and pride. After all we had been through, Jews had stood up for themselves and met respect rather than death!

As our numbers increased, it became more difficult to move around. Some in the Bielski partisans thought that we should not take in more people, for fear that our large number would give us away. But Tuvia proclaimed, "I want to be surrounded by thousands of Jews!" In one month, we grew from 25 to 150 people!

The Oppenheims, my relatives who had lived with us in the ghetto, were included in this group. My young cousin Miriam was pretty, with expressive brown eyes set in a thin, pale face framed by straight light brown hair. She looked scared and lost, the same way I looked when I first joined the partisans. My heart went out to her. She was only five years old and lived with constant fear, never knowing what might happen next. Even including her brothers, there were few children in our group, and none her age, so she had no one to play with, no toys, and no school to learn how to read and write. Miriam had only the clothes on her back and had to be satisfied with the food given to her, like the rest of us. Such difficult lessons for a young child!

I was pleased to have Miriam around and enjoyed playing with her. However, I was desperate for security and became convinced that I needed a gun for self-protection. Miriam's father, my Uncle Shmuel Oppenheim, came to my aid. I had begged the partisans to bring this family out of the ghetto to the forest, but because Uncle Shmuel was not a fighter and had a family that included a young child, some of the partisans had been against them joining our group. I had pleaded with Tuvia that, other than my father, I had no family of my own. My mother,

Shmuel Oppenheim. *Photo courtesy of the Jewish Resistance Museum, Novogrudek*

my sisters, and my brothers were gone. Tuvia, with his kind heart, overruled the other partisans.

A machinist by trade, Uncle Shmuel was a handy, resourceful man, and proved to be very helpful. He fixed all the guns and rifles and collected ammunition for both the Russian and the Jewish partisans. My uncle knew how fortunate he was and wanted to repay my kindness to his family, so he fashioned me a rifle (and later a gun) out of broken parts. Holding my own rifle for the first time, I felt safe in the midst of the terrible insecurity and fear that at times nearly took me over the edge of panic.

I learned how to use and service my rifle. Slung over my shoulder, it soon became part of me. A small group was organized to learn how to shoot. It did not occur to me until I looked around that day that I was the only female! A friendly, barrel-chested man who had been trained in the Polish army taught us step by step how to clean and maintain our guns, how to load, take aim, fire, and reload. I had had no previous interest in guns and knew nothing about them, but now felt compelled to learn everything I could.

It only took a week to feel entirely comfortable. My gun was my protector and a constant reminder of the fear I faced.

I went on guard duty, just like anyone else with a rifle. Guard duty was a solitary affair that involved long hours watching and listening. Many lives depended on the guard. It was scary to be alone as it grew dark, but I tried to remain calm and alert.

Slowly, I grew more attuned to my surroundings and came to know intimately the sounds of the forest. I learned to differentiate between the various birds' songs and even among the sounds of trees, pine and fir, birch and spruce. It brought to mind the summertime trips to the countryside my brother and I had taken with groups of Jewish children, where we had listened to stories and sung so many songs together. How gentle and peaceful the forest had seemed to me then!

Still beautiful, it was now fraught with danger, yet a feeling of safety enveloped me every time I saw the sun setting between the trees, for the Germans, governed by their own fears of ambush, did not attack at night.

I helped with the cooking and went on missions to obtain food, information, and supplies, and even to save lives. Women and girls rarely went on missions, as they did not usually possess arms. I believe that my friend, Itka—a girl I had first met in Bais Yakov Hebrew School in Novogrudek— and I were the only girls who did. Perhaps we were not as strong as the men, but we knew how to use our rifles. Equipped with a rifle and participating in missions, I was accorded a new sense of esteem from other partisans. I felt good to be able to help others in this way. Missions were dangerous, but it was an honor to go on them.

We had some narrow escapes. I was often scared for my life, but I felt safer than I might have otherwise because we were always in a group protected by one of my cousins. I recall how once, returning from a mission, we found ourselves in the midst of an *oblava* (raid). We ran deeper into the woods and then trekked through the swampy forest for days, but the Germans again discovered us. Fortunately, we kept our wits about us and quickly dispersed, so we lost them once more. We were lucky to survive. "God was watching over you," my father later told me.

I have to admit that I found the idea of revenge appealing, but this desire was always tempered by the knowledge of the price we had already paid: We did not always get away without losing someone.

At one point, we had settled in a forest close to the village of Stankievicz, the Bielskis' home village. When a German unit attacked us there, many partisans were killed, including Tuvia's wife, sister-in-law, and nephew. We did not see Tuvia for days and wondered how we could survive without his leadership, but finally he collected himself and returned to take charge. He led us to the forest of Nalibocka Pushcha and ordered us to break up into small groups and head further into the woods. There we regrouped, and Tuvia and a young engineer oversaw the building of *ziemlankas,* or bunkers.

NINE

1200 Jews in Ziemlankas

Ziemlankas became our homes, our sleeping quarters and places of refuge. We were lucky to have among us the engineer who designed these simple but useful structures. Each ziemlanka housed up to 30 people. Ultimately, 20 were built, dug deep into the ground, with low log walls resting on the surrounding forest floor and a wooden ladder leading down to the packed earth below. Branches strewn across the simple log roofs effectively hid the bunkers from view. We never cut down trees nearby the ziemlankas, so the forest functioned as natural camouflage as well. A few were built into ground that was too low-lying and flooded so badly that the inhabitants had to move, but this never happened to me.

We managed to keep warm at rudimentary hearths made of hardened earth and by sleeping close together. We slept on wooden planks, one alongside the next, with our heads to the wall and our feet to the wide aisle that ran down the center of the rectangular structure. Family groups stayed together. A young woman and her cousin slept on one side of me and my father on the other. We slept on mattresses made of straw under blankets taken from nearby farmers. At night, we lit kindling or twigs to use as flashlights when we needed to reach the area designated as the outdoor "bathroom," far from the bunker. I went to sleep to the sound of 24 people breathing, snoring, and gossiping in low voices.

In a few months, our new home looked like a small settlement. By now, we had reached a population of 1200! It was odd to live in the middle of the forest in a village of our own making, yet sometimes it almost felt like normal life. We even had a wedding. Jewish law recognizes a marriage as long as there are two witnesses, and we certainly had more than that! The forest itself was the *chuppah*, the canopy under which the bride and groom stood as my father conducted the ceremony, because he was recognized as a kind and religious man, he was asked to officiate. I was proud of the respect people had for my father.

While this pride remained, however, the illusion of normal life never lasted. Suddenly it would all come back full force: the war, the Nazis, the ghetto, and the loss of my mother, sisters, brothers, aunts, uncles, cousins, and so many people I had once known.

All partisans who did not possess guns, and therefore did not fight, were workers. For all of us, jobs were assigned according to ability and necessity. We expected a high level of performance from each other because everything was vital to our continued existence. We had shops for sewing, tannery, gun repair, and shoe repair. The workshops were built above ground in one area of the camp. There was a house for the doctor and a quarantine location about half a mile away for those who had contracted contagious diseases like typhus.

A kitchen provided food for everyone in the camp. All cooking was done outside, releasing pungent smells from soup simmering in large pots to waft among the trees. Once a day, people stood on a long but quickly moving line, talking casually together, holding plates and spoons in anticipation of the noonday meal. Occasionally, partisans brought back food from their missions. I recall once frying tons of potato pancakes made from potatoes that partisans had "captured" on their raids.

Milk collected from our 30 cows was an important staple of the partisan diet. Tuvia put my father in charge of the milk distribution, because the job required a person who was perceived by all to be absolutely fair. Since my father was a religious, moral man, he fit the role perfectly. I was proud that he was universally trusted and accepted. Our group was so well organized that we serviced other partisan groups in the neighboring forest, mostly the Russians, plus a little group of about 50 people. I felt honored to be part of the "town" my partisan group erected deep in the woods.

In addition, I was proud of my cousin Tuvia and what he was able to accomplish. Without any previous experience, he served as mayor, general, judge, diplomat, and friend, under difficult circumstances in difficult times. He had a group of bright, competent individuals who functioned as his cabinet, among them a lawyer, a doctor, and an engineer, as well as others capable of thinking clearly and working for the common good. Together, they helped Tuvia to make decisions and achieve goals.

The lawyer took upon himself a very dangerous mission, meeting with other partisan messengers in the densest part of the forest to share intelligence on the whereabouts and intentions of the German army. The doctor organized medical quarantines whenever there were infectious diseases, such as typhus and typhoid. Other members of the committee aided Tuvia in deciding what to do about the newly formed Jewish contingents of fighters who approached us with a view to joining, but were as yet without adequate experience in evading and fighting Germans.

All of these decisions had far-reaching effects on everyone in our *otriad* and could have easily caused friction and distracted us from our main goal: to survive and to fight the enemy. Yet the mutual respect of the three brothers inspired other cabinet members to act in the same fashion, enabling the committee to function wisely and well.

Of course, incorrect decisions were sometimes made, for unlike fairytale heroes, real people make mistakes. Nevertheless, we knew in our hearts that Tuvia and his group tried their best against all odds, and their word was ultimately accepted by all.

TEN

A Battle of Wits

$\mathcal{A}$t one point, we needed information about the whereabouts of the German army. I volunteered to obtain this information from the Russians, along with two men, one a little older than I, and another whom I'd known from my hometown. We took off through the *pushcha* (forest) in a horse and buggy early enough to arrive at the Russian-controlled *aerodrome* (airport) before nightfall. It was almost ten miles in each direction, a few hours each way, so it was a tiring trip, if relatively safe.

The so-called airport was little more than a rustic area cleared of trees and grass. We received our information from the Russians, who had received it in parachutes dropped down to them. One of the Russians gave me their last parachute as a parting gift. We put it to good use: our tailors sewed clothes from the material, and I knitted myself a sweater out of its silken threads.

Sometimes, it was hard to know whom to trust. A short time after the trek to the airport, my rifle had a cracked handle and I had to visit a small town nearby where there was a villager who could fix it. A few other partisans also had guns to be repaired and decided to make the trip with me. We borrowed a horse and buggy and began what I thought would be a routine trip.

After a ride through the forest, we arrived at the villager's home. We walked in, and much to our surprise, found a group of Russian soldiers in the process of assembling grenades to be detonated under railroad tracks to sabotage the Germans' transport of weapons and soldiers. They turned out to be partisans from the Stalin Brigade.

They immediately began to grill me: "Hello there, where are you from?" When I told them, one said, "Ah, the Bielski Brigade! You know, the Bielski partisans do nothing to help the war effort. They just care about saving Jews, not fighting the Germans."

"Yeah," said one of his companions, "they just hide out in the forest with their wives and girlfriends."

"Hey, are you someone's girlfriend?"

They knew just what to say to bait me, and I, being young, responded with indignation. "What are you talking about?" I snapped. "We came here to fix our rifles in order to shoot Germans!"

A handsome young commander smiled seductively, and swaggered toward me, "Well, Essie—is that your name?— come with us and help us blow up a railway bridge. That will prove you're a true partisan fighter!" I knew then I was trapped. I felt I had no choice but to go off with them, filled with regret at my foolish bravado.

I barely knew these men, and I was the only female, but the next day I crossed the *pushcha* in the company of these seven strangers, the only one of my original group to go. I began to feel even more uneasy, because they were preparing to face their ordeal by drinking. Passing the bottle back and forth, they continued to taunt me. "Oh, we will see what this Jewish girl is capable of!" "Let's see what kind of fighter she is!"

I became more and more nervous, more and more afraid of the Russian partisans who were supposed to be our friends. We came to the Niemen River and boarded a flat boat to go across the river. On the way over, one of the men became sick, probably due to his drinking. The others decided in disgust to leave him at the edge of the river when we landed. They didn't want to leave him alone, so one of the men turned to me and said, "Here's your way out. You stay with him!" I started to protest, but they left me there with their drunken comrade in the nearby home of a villager.

They returned several hours later in fine spirits. They had succeeded in blowing up the railway bridge, causing significant damage to the Germans in the process. They sang, yelled, and drank their way back to the village. When we arrived, the handsome commander pronounced, "OK, Essie, now you come with me!"

I knew that I could not be alone with this man, so I gushed, "Oh yes! I just need to get something first." I ran into the adjoining room, where I found a village girl about my age. I whispered, "We must get out of here. The men are drinking and it's not safe for you or me!" She quickly agreed and together we sneaked out a different door and spent the night at her neighbor's house.

The men were in a surly mood the next morning, preoccupied with recovering from their night of drinking, particularly the commander, who was angry that I had managed to escape him the night before. Afraid to try again, I felt once more that I had no choice but to go with them when they left the house.

Arriving at a small village in what seemed to me the middle of nowhere, for I have never had a good sense of direction, the commander casually said, "Essie, I'm very thirsty. Why don't you get me some water?" I went to a village house to get the water and returned to see the wagon disappearing into the distance, the hearty laughter of the Russian partisans just barely audible. The commander was jubilant: he had finally gotten the last word!

To my dismay, I had no idea where I was. It was certainly a very small village, but with my poor sense of direction, it took me a while to get my bearings. Finally, I struck out across a field of wheat and found the house where we had spent a night with the ferryman who had taken us across the river. The man was now cutting wood in the front of the house.

He glanced up when he saw me approach. In answer to my entreaty, he drawled, "Well, I took you along when you were with the Russian partisans, but not now." "Really," I said, "Why not?" The man just shrugged and returned to his task. I waited for him to look up again before I calmly pronounced, "You know, I have a gun." Staring at me, he slowly nodded, put down his axe, and took me across the river.

I climbed the riverbank and found the house of the villager who had agreed to repair my rifle. I strode into the house to retrieve my rifle and was shocked to see the same group of Russian partisans who had left me in the dust!

I was so angry that I cried out before I could think, "What is wrong with you? You left me in the middle of nowhere. I could have died out there, and you just took off without caring what happened to me! I'm a partisan, but what kind of partisan are you? I'm going to tell General Platon about you!" General Platon was the chief commander of the Russian partisans, and he had great respect for Tuvia and our group. I felt sure he would not regard this poor behavior lightly. I yelled so loudly that peasants ran in to investigate the commotion. I achieved two goals by this ruckus. First, I vented my anger, and second, I managed again to escape being alone with these men.

I spent the night in the villager's home and woke up before everyone else the next morning to make the long walk back to my partisan settlement, more relieved than ever to feel finally rid of the whole lot. On the way, I met up with a young doctor who had been visiting her boyfriend. She was on her way back to her base as well, so I didn't have to go alone and could take courage in her company.

Although our walk took one long day, I was in a good mood: I was going home, I had stuck up for the Bielski Partisans, and I had defended myself! I told myself with pride, "You're not a helpless girl, you're a partisan!"

Bielski Partisans guarding the Pushka airstrip
photo courtesy of the Bielski family

ELEVEN

Final Mission

$\mathcal{T}$hat was not my last mission, nor my last encounter with Russian partisans. Sometime later, Tuvia called a meeting of the partisans who owned weapons. Itka and I attended this important meeting.

"For the first time, we will fight the Germans face-to-face, without ambushes," he declared. "We will not run into the forest to hide." We listened in stunned silence. This was no longer guerilla warfare, but a very different approach to fighting from what we had learned, and far more dangerous. As Itka and I cleaned our rifles to prepare for battle, I whispered, "Itka, let's stick together, so we can keep safe from the Germans and the Russian partisans! After all, we're girls, and we don't want to be overpowered!" I had learned that, unless they were men we knew, it was dangerous to trust them, even if they were Russian partisan allies.

Itka and I drew strength from this pact to stay together, but my father became distraught and went to appeal to his nephew and commander. "Tuvia, I have already lost four children. Esia is the only child that I have left. Please don't send her on this dangerous mission."

Tuvia called me over and gently said, "Esia, you don't have to go, and if you decide not to join the unit, I will not take away your rifle." This was a most generous offer, because rifles were like gold; if someone was not using a weapon, it was given to a partisan who would use it.

I had to think hard, for I was torn. This mission was fraught with danger, even more than usual. I certainly didn't want to die, nor did I think my father would survive without me. I did not wish to go against my father's wishes, because I was taught to honor and obey my elders, and naturally, it was against my religion to kill except in self-defense. "Tuvia", I said, "I don't want an excuse. I want to go. This is my time to fight the Nazis." And so Itka and I went on the mission.

The plan was to fight a nearby German unit. We learned from the Russians that the Germans were in retreat and were trying to kill as many of us as they could in a final burst of rage as they were driven away.

However, even with Russian and Jewish partisans together, we were no match for the well-trained German army, and we had to go deeper in the forest. We crossed treacherous swamps, laying down logs and branches as we went along, trying to keep out of the muck by balancing precariously on our improvised road, where it would have been all too easy to fall in and drown. Once past the swamp, we fled through more thick forest.

The Russian and German armies crossed paths that day, and shot at us as we ran through their crossfire. We had to duck to avoid the bullets. We yelled in Russian, "We're partisans, don't shoot!" The Russian soldiers would stop, but the German soldiers continued to attack.

I was not hit, but other members of our group were not so lucky. One small boy from my town and nine men from the Bielski partisans were killed that day, and one woman, the mother of a friend of mine, was followed into a bunker, cornered, and shot. I thought to myself, "My father is right, it is better to live!"

TWELVE

The War is Over At Last

*T*hat turned out to be the last day of the war. It was over, really over. We left our forest home and traveled back to our towns, places that we had not seen for years. It took a day to walk to Novogrudek. I remember it all so clearly. Tuvia, Asael, and Zus riding ahead on their horses, looking like conquering heroes, true Maccabees, each with his own group of partisans returning to their towns. I tried to imagine what they were feeling and hoped they would remember the many wise decisions they had made and the 1200 lives they had saved, including my father's life and mine.

It felt unreal to walk without fear of reprisal. How could that be when fellow Jewish partisans had been killed just hours before? As we walked through the woods on our way to Novogrudek, I no longer looked and listened for a hidden enemy. I noticed the light flickering through the tall swaying trees.

It felt strange to have the luxury simply to appreciate nature. In peace, the woods brought back happy memories of my childhood, yet I could not shake sorrowful memories of my lost family, too. Overcome by the calm of the forest, I reveled in the healing power of nature.

As I walked toward my old home, I prayed that one day I would be able to share my story with a civilized world, a world without Nazis, without war, a world where children and all young people felt safe. I prayed that I would share my experiences so that they could learn from what I had gone through.

At last, we reached Novogrudek. It looked so different and yet the same. People seemed to be going about daily life as usual, but many of those we had known were no longer there. Some buildings were still standing, but many were gone. Things had disappeared. All that remained of our old life were pieces of wood and broken dishes, for anything of value had long since been stolen. We moved into my Uncle Yoshke's house and tried to begin again the business of living, but it was hard to do. My father and I had only each other: no personal possessions, no clothes, no photographs, no family jewelry, and no heirloom Passover goblet to celebrate Seder. We felt strange in our new existence, as if everything had been switched while we were dreaming and we had awakened once more to someone else's life.

My cousin Taiba and her husband lived with us at Uncle Yoshke's place. The first thing they wanted to do was to get their daughter back. Lola was now over three-and-a-half years old, and her Christian parents were the only ones she could remember. My cousin had to find Lola in the village where she was living, and then needed to locate a sympathetic neighbor who could assist her in recovering the child.

One day, the neighbor told Taiba that she herself would be taking care of Lola while the Christian parents were away. Taiba and her husband came to the village and used candy to entice Lola into their carriage, saying they needed her to show them the way to Novogrudek. The neighbor encouraged Lola to go with these strangers, so she did, but when Lola realized that they were not going to let her get out of the carriage, she cried and carried on. She had no idea who these people were who claimed to be her real parents, and she desperately wanted to get back to her familiar home. Taiba did everything she could to soothe her. How painful it must have been to have her own child not recognize her.

After a few weeks, one day there was a knock on the door. Before anyone realized what was happening, Taiba, in great distress, threw a blanket over Lola and carried her out the back door, down a small walkway, through a gate, and into an adjoining apartment.

Another time, I opened the door and Lola was amazed to see her adoptive parents standing there in front of her. She ran to them immediately. When Mr. Kenceizier bent down to pick her up, she flung her arms around his neck and wouldn't let go. When Taiba grabbed her from behind, Lola seized her adoptive father and held on for dear life. The screaming and crying that ensued was horrible, and Taiba and her husband were terrified of losing their child again.

Lola was very distressed, especially when she heard church

bells ringing. She would beg and plead to be taken to church. She was a baptized Christian and knew how important it was to go to church on Sundays.

No one would take her there. Desperate, she built a little altar in the corner of one room and prayed there. I saw what she was going through and felt so bad for her that I asked my cousin if I could take her to church. This took tremendous courage, for even after the war, it did not feel safe for a Jew to go into a church, but I could not bear to see Lola so sad. It seemed to comfort her to kiss the statues and to be in the surroundings she recognized and loved. But when I said to her, "Lola, they're only clay," she touched the statues as ordinary objects.

The entire experience of separation and reuniting was wrenching for everyone—her real parents, her adoptive parents, for my father and me, and of course for Lola herself. Finally, Lola accepted that her true parents had returned and that her adopted family would have to give her up. Lola lived entirely with the family she was born into and had no further contact with the Kenceiziers.

For my part, I immediately searched for the Foltanskis to thank them, but they were not to be found. Neighbors informed me that they had run away, because people who had worked for the Germans now feared for their own lives. A year later, I tried again, but was never able to find out what happened to them. I have always wished I could have told them how much their help and encouragement had meant to my father and me, and how they had helped to save my life.

I did find my third grade teacher and expressed my gratitude by presenting her a bar of soap, a very rare gift at that time. I also thanked the neighbor who had let me clean myself off in her house after the nights I had spent in the cornfield. Giving thanks to those who had risked their own lives to reach out to my father and me helped soothe my pain.

Villagers showed us where my brothers' bodies were, so we were able to rebury them in a Jewish cemetery. We visited the mass grave where my mother and sisters had died. I often found myself sitting on a nearby rock overlooking the grave to feel close to them and hold them in my mind. In this way, I kept them part of my daily life.

My father found a job in a Russian-owned store and eventually moved to the United States where he remarried and had one son. A few partisan friends and I, including Itka, went back to school to learn bookkeeping. Henya and her family did not survive the ghetto. The Oppenheim relatives eventually moved to Israel.

All five in the partisan group survived the forest encampment, but one brother, Asael, was drafted into the Russian army and he was killed in action. A sister, Estelle, and brother, Jashua, fled to Minsk when the war began, where they found safety. Of the nine brothers and two sisters, the Nazis killed two brothers with their parents. The four other Bielski partisans, Tuvia, Zus, Aron and Taiba, and their sister Estelle and brother Jashua ultimately moved to America to join their brothers Nathan and Walter who had moved to the U.S. before the war.

Like many others who lived through the war, my story is one of survival and loss. I experienced these horrific events in my youth. Looking back, I realize more than ever that no child should have to cope with the dilemmas I had to face: survival, guilt, and blame. While I believed in myself and managed to live through a combination of courage and chance, the fact is that others, also courageous, died simply because of bad luck. Others, indeed most, never had a chance at all. I have relived these painful experiences because I believe that this story should be told. It shows us that there is something remarkable about human beings, how they can start over and keep on going.

Memories dim, but we should never forget what happened so long ago. I pray that no child will have to endure this kind of horror again. I hope that the Jewish generations to come will never have to experience our tragic pain and loss. Let us never forget the Holocaust and the partisans who died fighting for Jewish honor.

—End—

Jerry Shor, Officer in the Polish Army,
Essie's husband who she met and married after the war.